This book is dedicated to My mom, sister, dad, and stepmom

for their support throughout the years.

Your Love has carried me through.

This book is especially dedicated to Jennifer Pereira.

Her support and enthusiasm fueled me to finish this book.

My heart soared with joy when I watched her read the initial draft.

Excitement is a contagion.

I would also like to thank her son, Joshua Pereira,

for reminding me of who I was when I was young!

Introduction

Why did I begin writing this story? What does this story mean to me? Some stories just need to be told, and some art just needs to be created. My best works of art/writing happen when I step aside and am a conduit for something greater than me. I want to take credit, but really can we ever take credit for our work? Nothing happens in a vacuum and we are all inspired by each other; this story is no different. It happened because I was inspired to draw a top hat and mustache on a lady, and then the whole story pushed itself out of me, quite intensely. For an entire month all I would talk about was this story. People would ask me how I was doing, and I would be confused because I felt as if I was in the story, and I didn't know how I was doing yet, the next pages were still being written! In the meantime I step out of my way and let the art create itself.

This is my gift: a fairytale for humanity. Yes, that seems grandiose, I know. I couldn't call it a fairytale for adults because of the implications, and also because I wanted children to read it too. I couldn't just call it a fairytale because then the adults would ignore it, so humanity was the only word that fit. Alas, it is also coming from me, a person who strives to appreciate humanity even in its darkest form. This is my gift to humanity, to remind me that I *love* humanity, even though it drives me nuts quite often! The raven is a continuous theme in this story, as is the lady in a top hat; both are archetypical tricksters (the lady because she has both masculine and feminine characteristics). I consider myself a trickster as well. It seems the only way I learn a lesson is by getting tricked into it. Much of my artwork also deals with this concept and I find that I am very focused on understanding trickery, or the trickster within me. I can't be sure!

This story is loosely based on the Major Arcana of the Tarot. The seasoned reader may recognize which pictures translate to which cards, but it is not necessary to enjoy the story. The tale is that of the fool's journey (or the hero's journey) in the way that I could relate to it. It is loosely based on personal experience, and then some on dreams!

Something that you may appreciate to know is the story that happened around this story. The day before I started doing the simple line drawings I was at the Long Beach WomanSpirit Faire, and saw a top-hat on sale. I had wanted that top hat for about three years! I was excited and started wearing it everywhere. The very next day I drew a picture of Dianna Agron wearing a top hat. Why, you ask? Because she had been asking people to draw Charlie (on her Tumblr account). It seemed interesting and some of the pictures I saw getting put up were cute, but not anything that I imagined Charlie to look like. On a whim, while at my desk job, I decided to do a quick line drawing of how I imagined Charlie. Because I associate Dianna with Charlie (as an alter ego) I used a picture of her to do the base 'female' image, and then I drew on a top hat and curly-Q mustache & goatee. After that the story just started unfolding itself in front of me, and it was all I could do to write it down and draw it out. I began the drawings/story on December 6, 2011, and finished on December 29, 2011. On December 31, 2011 I found a hurt raven in the middle of the road. I picked it up and took it to various animal hospitals, but they don't treat wild animals. I then took it home and gave it a place to rest and recuperate. It died in the night. I felt guilty and sad because it died, but in my dreams it came to me, and I realized we had created a bond; the raven would lead me through the New Year!

When I read books I never read the introduction; maybe because I'm impatient, or maybe because they can be rather long. So, I have tried to make mine short! I hope you enjoy this story. I thoroughly enjoyed living it for the month that I wrote it!

iii

A Fairytale for Humanity

By Giana Cicchelli

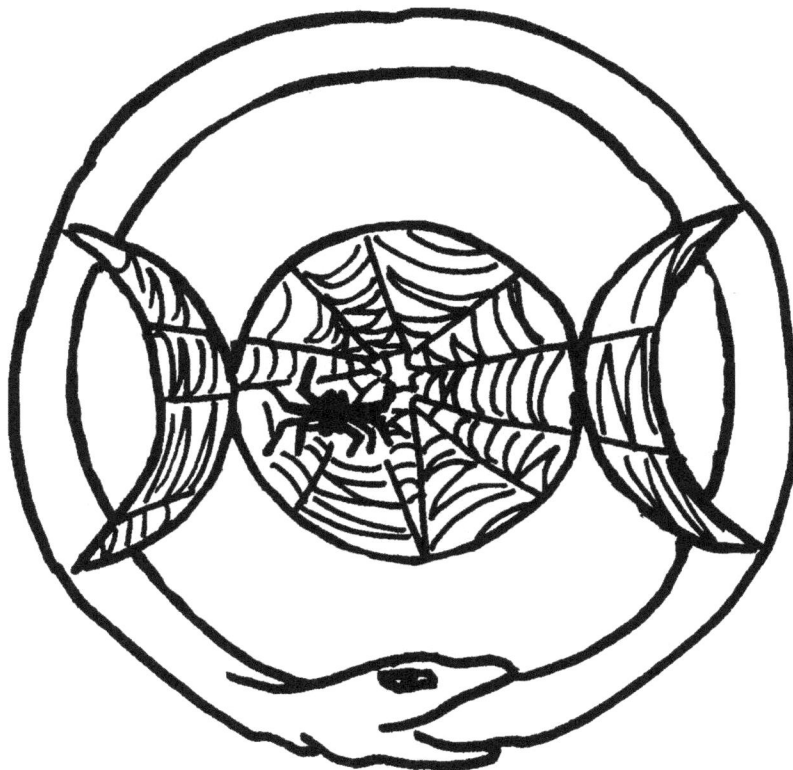

Our friendly trickster sets the stage...

One night during meditation our young heroine speaks to herself three years in the future about where they are headed.

"Further down the rabbit hole than you realize."

The response she got made her feel quite nervous, and rather young. In the midst of her fear a small gnome appears to help her along.

But, I am scared. Does Charlie know where to go?

The goal is actually to get lost, and then along the way you will find yourself.

"The road may get tricky, and you will be tested for authenticity. The only right answer is your own," says the gnome.

Reassured she decides to continue. Quickly on her way, filled with hope, she doesn't hear the gnome's parting words, "Easy though it may be, many have forgotten themselves along the path...."

In fact, the instructions seem so simple that her confidence decides to lead the way.

...And
so it began.

Come, come, whoever you are,
wanderer, worshipper, lover of leaving,
It doesn't matter.
Ours is not a
caravan of despair.
Come, come
even if you have
broken your vows
a thousand
times.
Come —
Come
yet again.
Come.

— Rumi

And So it Began.

Whilst walking towards her destiny the lady encounters another Lady, whose presence emanates a certain regal awe.

"Would you like to enter deeper into the mysteries?"

"I was following Charlie, and the gnome told me it would be better if I can get lost."

"Indeed, through these doors you can do just that."

"Why thank you kind lady. Is there anything I can do to repay you?"

"Yes. Listen closely to the beating of your heart, and contemplate *all* truths for at least a moment."

And with that the doors opened. Further mysteries beckoned our young heroine go forward.

As she continues she hears, "Listen closely to the beating of your heart," echo after her. Or was it within her? She couldn't tell.

Listen closely to the beating of your heart

13

Just barely through the doors she comes upon an artsy girl seemingly drawing her journey using simple lines and a black pen.

"What are you doing? Are you drawing me?"

"I am capturing beginnings! I am creating creation! I am documenting the hilarity of existence! Is it you? Hmmmm, I guess it might be!"

"Why are you..?"

"Because the only meaning is the one we create!"

The tiny gnome reappears, "Beware, a mile up there is a town that has many rules. You must walk quietly through, or be a very fast learner!"

17

Upon entering the town she notices a regal emperor with much allegiance throughout. She asks him, "Why?" To which he responds, "Creativity is the beginning of life, but for it to survive takes rules and order!"

19

As our young heroine begins to contemplate the Emperor's reality she remembers the beautiful Lady who beckoned her past the doors, "Contemplate all truths, if only for a moment, and lead with your heart."

Just then, at the exact moment that the thought billowed in her mind she heard the howl of a far off wolf.

A little startled she jumps, and whispers, "That was interesting! It was as if the universe was listening to my thoughts!"

At the same moment as she thinks this new thought there is a sudden burst of lightning.

Contemplate all
Truths, and Lead
with your Heart

Now feeling very unsure, she wonders, "Has the universe been listening all along?"

The silence of this reality echoes throughout her entire being. She shivers a little as she realizes the darkness has made her cold, and she forgot to bring provisions.

23

The gnome reappears and laughs heartily at her.

"Indeed, you have just learned one of life's ultimate truths, and that has chilled you to your very core. The universe *is* always listening to your thoughts, so *Think Carefully* ! There is a church ahead that gives refuge to travelers; there you will be warm throughout the night."

Think Carefully!

25

As she approaches the church she notices an old man out in the garden. He looks to be talking to the plants, but she can't be sure. It is dark, and she doesn't see as well at night. The old man calls to her as she gets closer, "Hello there young traveler. Are you looking for a place to stay the night? I am sure you are. The rosemary, here, has told me all about your journey. You are more than welcome."

"Did he say the rosemary told him?" she thinks to herself, but exhaustion takes over, and she can no longer be bothered to think through silly questions. She has a place to stay the night, and that is all that concerns her.

"I will show you to your chambers."

He Spoke to the Plants

27

In the night there is a ravenous wind. Swishing back and forth the leaves sound like rain, and our young heroine is pulled deeper and deeper into her dreams.

The beautiful Lady appears, again in front of doors, and asks, "Would you like to go deeper?"

"Didn't I already choose to go deeper?" she responds in confusion.

"Yes, however, if you go deeper still there will be no return to normal life. Are you prepared to face that consequence?"

It is your choice....

29

Feeling young and vulnerable she contemplates what that could possibly mean. She thinks, "Can I actually be held responsible for consequences when I do not yet know what they are!?"

"Of course" responds the Lady. Again shaken, she realizes that everyone can hear her thoughts! Even the rosemary knows her journey.

"Yes, I am ready to go deeper," she thinks, knowing everyone can hear her intention.

At the same moment she thinks her response she hears the crack of lightning and could swear she saw a smile creeping across the Lady's face. It was only but half a second after the sound that she realized the lightning wasn't far off.

The lightning had struck her head.

I am
Ready

33

Awake with a start she wonders, "Was that a dream?"

Before she can begin to revel in her latest quandary she notices a satyr outside her window. She can hear him beckon her into the night air, "Follow me into the night, the winds are whistling and the faeries are dancing."

His lips weren't moving but she could hear all of his words inside her head. She couldn't be sure how long she had slept; the night still has only the glow of moonbeams. She doesn't worry much more about it as she feels fully rested, and excited at the prospect of a night adventure.

"Follow me..." she hears, "follow me."

"Might as well," she whispers with a sigh, "might as well."

limbing out her window she is quite surprised that the wind is warm. The Satyr is far ahead prancing towards what looks like a swarm of fireflies. The music of his pipes is leading the way, and she follows easily. As she comes to where the music ends she realizes the Satyr is long gone, but amidst the roots of the tree are a circle of mushrooms with smiles on their faces and a song on their lips.

"Mushrooms don't have faces!" she thinks to herself. Again her thoughts are heard by all, and the mushrooms look at her with scorn, however, instead of replying they just keep on singing, ignoring her all the more. Still confused by the loss of the Satyr, she wonders where those fireflies must've gone. Looking around to see if they could be behind the tree, she doesn't realize, nor care, that she is walking directly into the mushroom circle. Alas, dear reader, she has never heard of faerie magick or tales of mushroom circles before, so how could she have known?

Immediately transported, she finds herself facing *Herself*. It was very strange, but comforting at the same time.

39

"Do I know you?" she asked of herself, immediately thinking that was probably the silliest question ever.

"I do not know you!" responded herself.

"What!?" she thought, "How could this be? This lady here is clearly me!"

Hearing her thoughts, and concerned with the truth herself replied, "I am not you! Or at least you have led me to believe that I am not, all along."

"Pardon, have we met before?" she asks herself.

"Not really. You have never acknowledged my existence." At the exact moment that the words are spoken she looks at the clothing that Herself is wearing. Those are clothes that she would be too afraid to strut around in.

She also notices other little things that she had only had the vaguest thought about before deciding that it was something she *could not* do.

"Oh my! You are me. You are the me that I have never allowed myself to be!" she exclaims, the realization striking her head like another bolt of lightning.

"Indeed. I am the parts of you that you refuse to acknowledge. Now that we've officially met, I must say I will be rather perturbed if you continue to ignore me!"

"That shall be easy, now that we have met!" she replies, but just as she says it a wave of fear washes over her, "Oh my! But I am afraid to be the parts of me that are you! I don't know how I can wear those clothes, or think those thoughts!"

"You realize you are talking to yourself, do you not? Then I will let you in on a little secret, if you continue to ignore me I will grow stronger, fiercer, and angrier than you can even imagine. I will slowly cast a shadow upon your waking life that will have you living in a state of fear that I do not wish on my enemies. The shadow will eventually grow so large that it will eclipse who you *think* you are. Eventually I will get out, one way or another." Herself says with a wink.

Stronger, fiercer, Angrier!

43

In that instant she was alone and herself had disappeared.

"But I am afraid," she thought, "I am afraid! What if people don't like me?"

45

This last thought was so loud that the whole night sky echoed with it. She closed her eyes to swim in the echo.

what if...

47

When she reopened them, there were faeries dancing all around her singing, "Heed our magick my sweet dear, listen to our song, heed the story of yourself, and remember to sing along!"

They sang as a great choir might sing, full of joy but tinged with the intensity of urgent truth.

Listen to Our Song

A great wind blows through her thoughts, and the faeries are whisked into a turning circle as if a joke. She laughs, and the faeries giggle with her, and then they sing eerily, "Times, they are a changing!" and with that they are gone. The silence comforts her insecurities; she decides to walk a bit.

Times, they are a Changing!

51

Hours had passed in the darkest part of night, and our young heroine was entranced by the quiet of her mind. She was in full absorption of all that had happened since her meditation and yet not thinking a single thought.

Up ahead there were lights, laughing and revelry; the sound snapped her out of her solitude. She decided that she was ready for another adventure, even if she wasn't actually sure that she was.

Knocking on the cottage door she wonders if it may be rude for her to interrupt, but before she can give it much mind the door swings open, "There you are! We have been waiting!!"

"You have been waiting for me? But I was following Charlie, or at least that's where I began…" she says, realizing how much of her own story she has already forgotten.

"Indeed, I am Charlie!" he exclaims. And indeed, he was wearing a top hat and had a mustache, but she thought Charlie's features were more feminine.

"Never mind you with my features, I appear differently to people at different times!" he says with a wink. The music gets louder and she looks past the front door and sees that everyone is singing and dancing.

"What fun that must be," she thinks to herself.

"Welcome to my home," Charlie says as he opens the door more for her to enter.

We
have
been
Waiting.

57

"Oh! How very pretty you are," Charlie remarks.

"Why thank you!" she answers, quite surprised. She didn't realize until exactly that moment that she had never thought herself pretty.

Still in revelry of this realization, and happy to be recognized as such she didn't see that the group had begun dancing around her, in a circle they chanted and continued to sing, hopping, skipping and jumping to the rhythm.

59

"And my dear your energy is so very strong, you are enchanted, and have magick running in your veins!"

"Magick? Like the faeries?" twirling now too, she had been swept into the circle.

"Yes, like the faeries, but oh, how much more powerful than them you are! You are so very special in so many magnificent ways."

The compliments were making her feel light and shiny, like she could fly, and when she looked around she saw that she was actually flying, three feet in the air, in what seemed to be a whirlwind. In the commotion she heard more and more compliments circle around her, and she thought that she may like to be complimented all her life.

You are
so
very
special.

61

The thought had just entered her head when she fell to the floor.

"You, you mustn't lose your concentration!" Charlie retorted tersely to her falling, "It is your fault that you fell, and I will not stand for you to do it again!"

"But I don't know what happened!" She replies, embarrassed, "How can I be to blame if it was not my choice to go up in the first place!?"

"It was your choice, and your desire, to fly to the very reaches of the sky on the accolades of your greatness; however, you will never make it that high if you think like that! And my goodness, what are you wearing? That will never do. I must fashion you in my image."

With each critique she felt herself get smaller and smaller, until when she looked around everyone seemed twenty feet tall, and they were all looking down on her. They began their song and dance again, this time going the opposite direction and with a more somber tune. The song matched the words, as they continued to tromp around her, "Glutton, Selfish, Lazy, Ugly, Immature" The words, the words circling her, taking her to the low that reminded her of the opposite of flying.

azy! Selfish! Glutton! Ugly!
is your fault! It is your fault!
utton! Selfish! Lazy! immature!
Lazy! Immature! You don't know anything! worthless!
you are a shivering child

63

"STOP!!" she yelled. At once she was regular size and she could see that Charlie was not actually Charlie at all. He was wearing a top hat and had a mustache, but there was a sharpness to his nose and eyes that reminded her of a shark, "You are not Charlie! You are a liar, and a charlatan!"

"Do you even know who Charlie is?" Sneered the imposter, "No, you don't! You cannot remember anything about why you began this journey, or even where you started. You are a sniveling child that pretends to understand the world."

She thought to herself for a moment, and asked, "Where did I start this journey? And where was I going? What is my purpose?"

"Well, those big questions for that pretty little head of yours must be quite scary. Don't you worry my pretty little dear, stay here with me and I will make sure that everything you could ever need is provided."

He didn't look as much like a shark now, but his face was changing rather dramatically in such a short time span. "Could she live like this, with a person who was so mercurial? Did she deserve more?" she thought to herself, hoping no one was listening.

64

"Of course you deserve more!" said the gnome, but she could not see him in the house, "I am with you in spirit my dear! You are an amazing lady, and you have so many beautiful things to do in this life. Do not trade in your possibilities for a life of empty promises and parlor tricks!"

67

"If you leave now, you will never be great! You will never make your mark on this world! You will never be anything but a sniveling child!"

"I am leaving." She states sternly, looking the man square in the eyes, "I am leaving, and I am leaving right now. Even if your lies were the truth, I would not stay here and suffer with you!"

Something in the tone of her voice made her seem so much taller than she had been when she entered the house, and with this burst of strength the man cowered in the corner and looked away; she was free to leave.

I am Leaving Right Now.

69

Outside, she takes a deep breath, and exhales all her tension, "That sure was a close one!" she thinks to herself, "but I must always remember that though he wasn't who he said he was, he still had some valid questions; what am I looking for? Who is, and why am I looking for, Charlie? When did I begin this journey? I have been very content to walk into one adventure after another, but what is *my* adventure?"

"Very good," says the gnome, as he appears to her, "very good indeed! Many will never discover this aspect of the truth!"

"Well that is fine, and good, but what do I do now?" she replies rather sincerely.

"It depends on what you would like the story of your life to read as; if you were reading this story, what would you want to see happen next? Until now you have been blindly led without any real understanding of where you're going or where you began."

"Hmmm, I have never asked myself what my story would be! This is very interesting. I suppose it is not enough to continue to seek out the mysteries of life, is it?"

"Yes, you may dedicate your life to only that, but that dedication can be intertwined with your life story, as it is now, or it can be the main plot! Your choice," he responds with a wink, and with that he is gone.

How would you like the story of your life to Read?

73

"Oh dear! My choice! And what a choice indeed! What will I want people to remember about me? That charlatan had told me that I have great things to do in this life, and I imagine that was actually the truth; why else would he try to trap me so quickly!? I have always wanted to be a writer, and a poet, or maybe an artist like the girl who was drawing me before. I wonder why she is drawing me! That was very peculiar! Maybe I shall be a leader in government, or a mother, or a fortune teller!" her thoughts were rambling on in every which way.

President?
writer?
Poet?
artist?
Mother?
Leader?
fortune
teller?
astronaut?
Philosopher?

"So many options, my dear," interrupts the Lady, "many, many options and yet no clear focus of who you are. *Who are you?*"

"Well, I am not sure. I am a lady, that I know, and I love adventure, but who exactly am I or could I be?" she responds, quite perplexed.

"You have confined yourself to what you think you should be. The question is what is your deepest desire in the deepest darkness of your soul? I am sure you will recognize it once you find it! I imagine you thought of it briefly in your childhood!"

"But..." she responds looking towards that Lady, who was now also gone.

"Geez! So much coming and going, mixed with cryptic advice! I feel the need for a nap." She exclaims, whilst looking upon the ground for a place to rest.

Luckily there was a nice little soft patch tucked away behind a tree, and our young heroine could do just that.
In her dreams she saw the charlatan trying to tear her down, and the gnome and the Lady giving her advice, but all of their words were a jumbled mess, and she couldn't understand any of it.

79

Then she was face to face with herself. Initially a little frightened, for their last conversation had been rather tense, she was relieved when Herself smiled.

"Hello my sweet girl," herself cooed, "would you like some help dreaming the answer?"

"I would, I desperately would! I have no idea who I am!" she replies earnestly.

"I know. That is because you have never stopped to look at me, you have never truly let yourself experience your desires. What is it that you desire deep within yourself?"

Let your
Dreams
help
you.

81

"What do I want to be? What is my deepest desire in this life?" she thought. Deep within herself she kept hearing all the possibilities of who she could become, and she remembered the gnome saying that until now she had let herself be led instead of taking the reins.

Herself interrupted her thoughts to ask, "Is it really a title that you want to be? Or is it a feeling?"

83

"What?" she replied, quite confused. As she thought again about all the things that she could become, she thought, that she didn't want to pick only one.

She wanted to be everything in this life that she could be. She wanted to be a philosopher, a painter, a housewife, a palm reader, and the President! The sky was the limit, and she wanted it all! So if it wasn't a thing that she wanted to be, then it must be an overarching feeling. What did she want more than anything in this life?

At a moment everything became brighter in her mind and she knew; more than anything she wanted to be the heroine, she wanted to be the one that people looked to in awe, she wanted to be the moral of the story, she wanted to be recognized for all the hard work she put in and all the struggles that she had surpassed.

She wanted it all; she wanted to be the heroine of her own story!

"Well, being the heroine is a noble feat, but what must you do to become the heroine?"

"Make the right decisions?" she asked hesitantly, hoping it would be that easy (as if making the right decision would always be easy).

"Making the right decision is usually decided by the narrator. Generally a decision is made 'right' by how you tell the story. What you need to do to become the heroine is to decide what you are working towards, what you want to give to humanity. You must take the reins and rush forward with all your personal impetus! You must not wait; you must take action and know!" Herself said, as if speaking to a great auditorium.

"Yes!" she replied to herself, "I can do this!"

"One last thing," herself whispered, knowing that she wouldn't fully understand yet, "To be great you must be *brave* enough to do what sings in your heart, even if people tell you that it really isn't that good, they are speaking from expectation and not revelation."

The word revelation echoed throughout her whole body, reverberating her out of the dream. "I know what I must be," she whispered, "I must give life to all the thoughts and ideas that I have be afraid to share, I must give life to my humanity!"

Revelation...

As soon as it was said the moon eclipsed, and she was in darkness.

The darkness seemed so scary, and looming. She looked all around her and there was only darkness, she didn't even know which way to continue her journey; with darkness every which way she didn't know which way the light would be. She decided to just walk forward for as long as she could. When she got tired she lay down to sleep, and even though it was dark everywhere it was still warm so she felt she didn't need a blanket. The sleep was easy, for she was exhausted.

When she awoke it was still dark and so she continued forward hoping for light to appear somewhere. She went like this for days, for weeks, just walking forward in the dark. In all this dark she was able to think about all the things that she learned on this journey, she was alone, but she didn't feel alone, just very dark.

One day whilst walking she saw a glimmer of light up ahead. Just a glimmer, and very dim indeed, but still a light, or she thought it was a light. It disappeared so she wasn't sure she had actually seen it at all.

She contemplated all the things she must work towards in this life to become her own heroine. She formulated ideas, and took mental notes of concepts that people weren't always aware of.

93

When she ran out of interesting thoughts she found that the darkness got darker, and now she felt so very alone. When there was no light shining on things that could distract her she was forced to delve deeper into the recesses of her solitude. Buried below the various surfaces of her sociality were wounds and sadnesses that she had forgotten. They were still there growing even without the food of her thoughts. She saw anger she had never released and tears that had never been shed.

With the darkness becoming a sanctuary she gave up control, and allowed herself to feel everything that had been hidden deep within her. Her tears felt like the release of the weight of centuries, and suddenly she was crying for the stories of her ancestors that she wasn't even aware she knew. With her tears the rain began to fall, and in unison she and the earth were washed clean.

95

Suddenly, the light came back on. Just as abruptly as it had disappeared it reappeared. She hoped that it would stay, that the light wouldn't leave again.

The gnome reappeared and told her, "You have done a very good job! Yes, there will be times when it is dark but now you know how to get back to the light. Many get lost in the dark because they lose faith that the light will reappear and they stop their journey. As long as you have faith and continue on the journey you will be able to push through, and the light will reappear. Remember this always! You will be tested with this again."

Many get lost in the dark because they lose faith...

The gnome, again, was gone. One of the questions that had resurfaced over and over in the darkness, and that she could not seem to answer was, "who is Charlie? Why had she begun this journey following an idea in a top hat?"

Something in the look of the top hat had inspired her to go deeper into the mysteries than she could have ever imagined. When she had begun talking to her future self in meditation she had had Charlie in mind and she knew now that this shadow of a person had inspired all of her questions.

Who is Charlie??

"Still, did it really matter who Charlie was now that she was the master of her path?" she thinks rhetorically. Quickly, she decides that the matter of Charlie is no longer of any importance. She is on the journey now, and that was all that mattered. "Further down the rabbit hole than you realize," echoed through her mind, "Oh! Indeed," she whispered with a grin, "and further still, I imagine!"

And further still

She had spent so much time in the dark formulating her creation, and her creativity, that she had almost forgotten the words of the emperor, "Creativity is the beginning but for it to survive takes structure."

She wanted to give structure to her story, to her becoming. As she walks she notices a path, and decides to tread a path that was already taken. There was something so mundane about a path that it became sacred just to follow it. Along the path she thinks, "It seems surreal to be following expectations! There is nothing so scary about a trodden path!" These thoughts of safety reminded her of fear, "Such a funny thing fear is! To think I had been afraid of the emperor. I imagine I will fear nothing the same since I have met the charlatan!"

Indeed dear reader, once fear is overcome it becomes much easier to ignore in the future.

Something so mundane that it became sacred just to follow it . . . . . .

Up ahead there was a small market and she realized that they must have the tools she would need to create.
Seeing a store with art supplies and paper she thinks she would like to write her story down and express herself through art.
Looking through the different types of pens and markers she leaps a little when she sees a top hat at the end of the isle. "A top hat!! My dear, how interesting! I have always wanted one of those."

D eciding to try it on she thinks it would be funny to use one of the markers to draw on a mustache, "Maybe I will look like Dali!" she excitedly whispered. Behind the hat is a mirror. Trying it on, and stepping closer to the mirror to draw on a mustache, she couldn't believe what she was seeing! She was Charlie; she had been Charlie all along!

"I have been following myself deeper into myself?" she thought, "how silly of me, and yet how very appropriate!"

athering the tools she would need to make her story, she delighted in the fact that no one paid her fake mustache any notice, "how very peculiar!" she thought.

"No one notices an oddity if the oddity doesn't truly believe itself odd!" laughed the gnome, "I see you are ready to create your story, and you have all the materials you need. But my dear heroine, who are you?"

.......No One notices an oddity if the oddity doesn't believe itself odd....

"Who am I?" she thought again, this time more playfully, for now she knew.

"I am you, dear reader, I am you. This story will always be our journey."

The End

www.ingramcontent.com/pod-product-compliance
Lightning Source LLC
Chambersburg PA
CBHW081239020426
42331CB00013B/3226